Dear Friend,

Delight your family & friends with delicious handmade food gifts from our tried-&-true farmhouse kitchen recipes! Whether you need a hostess gift, a welcome basket for a new neighbor, or take-home treats for a child's party, these cleverly packaged food gifts are sure to please. Try your hand at crafting a no-sew fabric gift bag for a Soup Mix, an oh-so-easy paper sleeve for a loaf of fresh-baked Apple Bread or a one-of-a-kind serving dish for a Chocolate Cheese Ball. You may even want to mix and match foods and containers to create your own uniquely tasteful gifts...so many ways to show you care!

From our creative home to yours,
Vickie & Jo Ann

LEISURE ARTS, INC.
Little Rock, Arkansas

Farmhouse Apple Bread
A mouth-watering treat!

3 eggs, beaten
2 c. sugar
1 c. oil
1 T. vanilla extract
3 c. all-purpose flour
1 t. baking soda
1 t. cinnamon
3 to 4 apples, cored, peeled
   and chopped
1 c. chopped pecans

Combine eggs, sugar, oil and vanilla until well mixed; set aside.

Combine flour, baking soda and cinnamon in a separate bowl; stir into egg mixture. Fold in apples and pecans. Divide equally between 2 greased and floured 9"x5" loaf pans. Bake at 325 degrees for 50 minutes to one hour. Makes 2 loaves.

Bread Sleeve & Tag

- cellophane-wrapped Farmhouse Apple Bread
- decorative-edged scissors
- parchment paper
- scrapbook paper
- double-sided tape
- assorted ribbons, trims and rickrack
- craft glue
- cardstock
- $1^{1}/_{2}$"x$2^{1}/_{2}$" write-on self-adhesive labels
- buttons
- $4^{1}/_{8}$"x$9^{1}/_{2}$" vellum envelope

Bread Sleeve

For each sleeve, measure the circumference of your loaf and add 2". Use decorative-edged scissors to cut a 5" wide strip of parchment paper and straight-edged scissors to cut a $4^{1}/_{2}$" wide strip of scrapbook paper this measurement. Overlapping the short edges, wrap the layered papers around the loaf and secure with tape. Tie lengths of ribbons, trims and rickrack around the sleeve.

Tag

For each tag, glue scrapbook paper to cardstock and cut a $3^{1}/_{8}$"x4" rectangle. Adhere a label to a piece of cardstock. Cut the cardstock $1/_{8}$" larger on all sides than the label. Loosely sew a button to one end of the tag; glue rickrack and the cardstock label to the opposite end. Tie lengths of trim around the button. Write your desired message on the tag.

To make two pouches, seal an empty vellum envelope; then, use decorative-edged scissors to cut a $3^{1}/_{4}$" high section from each end of the envelope. Insert a tag into each pouch.

Greet a new neighbor with a gift of freshly baked Farmhouse Apple Bread. Wrapped in a decorative sleeve of scrapbook paper with a hand-lettered tag, this delicious treat from your kitchen is sure to say "Welcome."

Heartfelt Thanks

It's been said that good things come in small packages and that is certainly true of these mini loaves of Almond-Lime Bread. The tasty confections are just the right size for individual thank you gifts for co-workers, neighbors or friends.

Bread Sleeve & Tag

- cellophane-wrapped Almond-Lime Bread
- decorative-edged scissors
- scrapbook paper
- buttons
- double-sided tape
- cardstock
- craft glue
- ribbon and rickrack
- hole punch

For each sleeve, measure the circumference of your loaf and add 2" for overlap. Use decorative-edged scissors to cut a 2" wide strip of scrapbook paper this measurement. Sew a button to the center top of the sleeve. Overlapping the short edges, wrap the strip around the loaf and secure with tape.

For each tag, cut a 2½"x3" rectangle from cardstock. Center and glue a 2"x2½" scrapbook paper rectangle to the cardstock; then, add a length of ribbon. Write your message on the tag and punch a hole in one corner. Use rickrack to tie the tag to the button.

Almond-Lime Bread
A great combination of flavors!

3-oz. pkg. lime-flavored gelatin, divided
3 c. buttermilk biscuit baking mix
½ c. sugar
¾ c. sour cream
½ c. milk
2 eggs
1 c. sliced almonds, divided
2 T. hot water
1 c. powdered sugar
¼ t. almond extract

Reserve one teaspoon lime gelatin for glaze. Combine baking mix, sugar and remaining gelatin in a medium bowl. Add sour cream, milk and eggs; beat until well blended. Stir in ¾ cup almonds. Spoon batter into 3 greased and floured 5½"x3" loaf pans. Bake 40 to 45 minutes or until a toothpick inserted in center of bread comes out clean. Cool in pans on wire rack 10 minutes. Remove bread from pans and transfer to a wire rack with waxed paper underneath.

For glaze, combine reserved one teaspoon gelatin and hot water in small bowl; allow to stand 5 minutes. Add powdered sugar and almond extract to gelatin mixture; stir until smooth. Drizzle glaze over warm bread. Sprinkle remaining ¼ cup almonds over glaze. Allow glaze to harden. Store in an airtight container. Makes 3 loaves.

Almond-Lime
Bread

Fun Party Pops

Surprise the children at your next get-together with a paddle ball treat party favor. After the tasty Chocolatey Rice Pops are consumed, the timeless toy will provide hours of old-fashioned fun.

Chocolatey Rice Pops
Kids of all ages will go for these!

3 T. butter
10-oz. pkg. marshmallows
6 to 7 c. crispy rice cereal
12 wooden treat sticks
6-oz. pkg. semi-sweet chocolate
   chips, melted
$1/2$ c. white chocolate chips, melted

In a large saucepan, melt butter over low heat. Add marshmallows; cook and stir until melted. Remove from heat; stir in cereal until well-coated. Press evenly into a lightly greased 13"x9" baking pan. Cool slightly; cut into 12 bars. Insert a stick into each bar; place on wax paper to cool.

Dip bars into melted chocolate to coat; let cool slightly and drizzle with melted white chocolate. Makes one dozen.

Tip: Melt chocolate chips in a double boiler over hot water, or in a microwave-safe bowl (microwave on high for one minute, stir and microwave an additional 15 seconds as needed). Stir until smooth.

Fun Party Pops instructions are on page 40.

Garlic-Romano Dipping Sauce

This sauce is also delicious over vegetables.

1 c. grated Romano cheese
1/4 t. red pepper flakes
1/2 c. olive oil
1 clove garlic, pressed
1 loaf Italian bread, cubed

   Whisk together cheese, red pepper flakes, oil and garlic in a small bowl; mix until well combined. Refrigerate until ready to serve. Bring sauce to room temperature before serving with bread. Makes 3/4 cup.

Denise Mainville
Huber Heights, OH

Break Bread Together

Farmhouse charm abounds from this tea towel-lined basket filled with Garlic-Romano Dipping Sauce, a loaf of crusty bread and an eclectic collection of red transferware bread plates. This quick and easy gift is sure to please!

Dipping Sauce Jar & Tag

- jar of Garlic-Romano Dipping Sauce
- decorative-edged scissors
- cardstock
- scrapbook paper
- 1³/₈" x 1³/₈" metal-rimmed tag with brads
- craft glue
- assorted trims (we used ribbon, twill tape, rickrack and lace edging)
- 1¹/₈" diameter button
- hole punch
- 1⁵/₈"x3" hang tag
- basket
- tea towel
- red transferware bread plates
- a loaf of bread in a brown paper bag tied with string

Dipping Sauce Jar & Tag instructions continue on page 40.

A Sweet Surprise

When traditional salsa and corn chips just won't do, try sweet and tangy Apple-Berry Salsa & Cinnamon Chips. Embellish the jar, bag and tag with embroidered motifs cut from vintage linens to make this duo as delightful to the eyes as they are to the tastebuds.

Chip Bag, Tag and Salsa Jar

- Apple-Berry Salsa in a clear glass lidded jar
- Cinnamon Chips in a cellophane bag
- scrapbook paper
- 5$\frac{1}{4}$"x8$\frac{1}{2}$" brown paper bag with handles
- craft glue
- assorted trims (we used ribbon and twill tape)
- vintage embroidered linens
- 1$\frac{3}{8}$" diameter button to cover
- decorative-edged scissors
- cardstock
- 2$\frac{1}{2}$"x4" hang tag
- $\frac{5}{8}$" diameter button
- cardboard
- batting
- self-adhesive hole reinforcements
- hole punch

Match wrong sides and glue two 7"x10" pieces of scrapbook paper together. From prepared paper, cut one bag topper 6$\frac{1}{4}$"x7" and one jar label 4"x2$\frac{1}{2}$".

Chip Bag

Match short ends and fold the bag topper in half; crease. Open the topper and cut a 4" long (or width needed to slip over your bag handles) slit along the center of the crease. Glue ribbon and strips cut from scrapbook paper across one short end of the topper for the front. Follow manufacturer's instruction to cover the button with an embroidered scrap. Center, then sew the button to the topper front. Place the Cinnamon Chips in the bag and slide the topper over the handles.

Tag

Photocopy the Cinnamon Chips label, page 45, onto cardstock and cut out using decorative-edge scissors. Glue the label to the hang tag. Embellish the tag with motifs cut from the embroidered linens, ribbon and a button. Hang the tag from the button on the topper.

Salsa Jar instructions are on page 40.

Apple-Berry Salsa & Cinnamon Chips

A tried & true recipe!

2 apples, cored, peeled and chopped
1 c. strawberries, hulled and coarsely chopped
1 to 2 kiwis, peeled and coarsely chopped
zest and juice of 1 orange, divided
2 T. brown sugar, packed
2 T. apple jelly

Combine apples, strawberries, kiwis and zest in a large bowl. Mix juice, sugar and jelly in a small bowl; add to fruit. Serve immediately, or chill until ready to serve. Serve with cinnamon chips. Makes 8 servings.

Cinnamon Chips:
non-stick vegetable spray
6 8-inch flour tortillas
6 T. sugar
1 T. cinnamon

Spray both sides of each tortilla with non-stick vegetable spray. Slice each tortilla into 8 wedges. Combine sugar and cinnamon in a large plastic zipping bag. Place tortilla wedges in bag; seal and shake to coat. Arrange wedges on a lightly greased baking sheet. Bake at 375 degrees for 8 to 10 minutes, or until crisp and golden. Makes 4 dozen.

Gigi Berrett
Orem, UT

A Memorable Treat

Are you the lucky recipient of some odd bits of Grandma's china and glassware? Turn those cherished pieces into a memorable gift for a family member by creating a one-of-a-kind serving dish to hold a Chocolate Cheese Ball. The secret to joining the overturned goblet and dinner plate is double-sided foam mounting tape! The tape holds the pieces securely but will not harm the china or glass and it can easily be removed if desired. A vintage silver butter spreader with ribbon accents makes the perfect serving utensil.

Vintage silverware pieces, like our butter spreader, are easily found in antique shops and flea markets. You may even have some of Grandma's old silverware tucked away in the attic or in a silver chest! Including a unique serving utensil with a food gift adds an extra special touch.

Card

Cut a 6³/₄"x9³/₄" rectangle from cardstock. Matching short edges, fold the rectangle in half. Cut a 6³/₄"x4⁷/₈" rectangle from scrapbook paper. Glue the scrapbook paper rectangle to one side of the card for the front. Use decorative-edged scissors to trim the short ends of a 2"x5³/₄" strip of scrapbook paper. Sew the scrapbook paper strip to the center of the front. Tie short lengths of ribbon through the holes of wooden alphabet letters that spell your special message; then, glue the letters onto the sewn rectangle. Glue strips of scrapbook paper and ribbon to the front, just above the bottom edge; then, sew a button to the center of the trim.

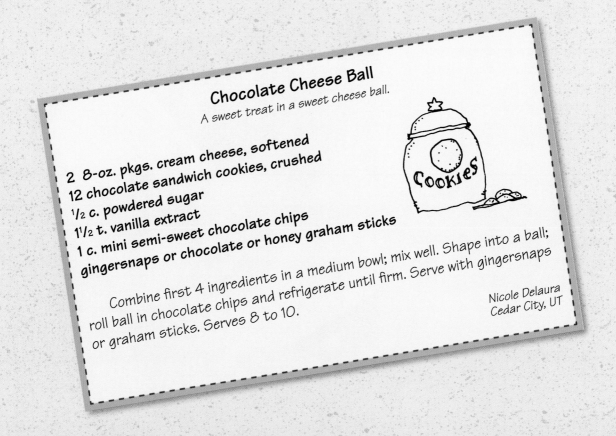

Chocolate Cheese Ball
A sweet treat in a sweet cheese ball.

2 8-oz. pkgs. cream cheese, softened
12 chocolate sandwich cookies, crushed
¹/₂ c. powdered sugar
1¹/₂ t. vanilla extract
1 c. mini semi-sweet chocolate chips
gingersnaps or chocolate or honey graham sticks

Combine first 4 ingredients in a medium bowl; mix well. Shape into a ball; roll ball in chocolate chips and refrigerate until firm. Serve with gingersnaps or graham sticks. Serves 8 to 10.

Nicole Delaura
Cedar City, UT

A Peach of a Gift

Spiced Peaches have long been a family favorite for special holiday dinners. Share the tradition with a hostess gift of a jar of Spiced Peaches. Nestle it in a basket lined with gingham fabric and a vintage embroidered napkin. A handcrafted tag adds the finishing touch.

Spiced Peaches

This recipe needs to be made 4 days ahead to allow favors to blend.

4 16-oz. cans sliced
   peaches in syrup
2 c. sugar
1 c. cider vinegar
4 4-inch cinnamon
   sticks, broken into pieces
2 t. whole allspice
2 t. whole cloves

Combine all ingredients in a large saucepan over medium heat; bring to a boil. Reduce heat and simmer, uncovered, for 30 minutes or until liquid is slightly thickened. Let cool.

Pour into a covered container. Refrigerate at least 4 days prior to serving. Remove from refrigerator approximately one hour before serving. Serves 8.

Kimberley Bercaw
Ewa Beach, HI

Spiced Peaches Jar & Tag

- Spiced Peaches in a clear glass lidded jar
- basket
- gingham fabric to fit basket, hemmed on all edges
- decorative-edged scissors
- embroidery floss
- assorted buttons
- craft glue
- assorted trims (we used ribbon, twill tape and rickrack)
- 3"x5" poster board tag
- two embroidered napkins
- cardstock
- scrapbook paper

Jar

Make a photocopy of a section of your gingham fabric. Using decorative-edged scissors, cut a circle from the photocopy slightly smaller than your jar lid. Use floss to sew a button to the center of the paper circle; then, glue the circle to the jar lid.

Cut a length of twill tape and rickrack long enough to wrap around the neck of your jar with a 1/2" overlap. Sew or glue the rickrack to the center of the twill tape. Glue the twill tape around the jar.

Tag instructions are on page 40.

A Dessert They'll Dig Into

Bring back fond memories of summer days spent building sandcastles at the beach or lakeshore with a Bucket-of-Sand Cake. Use twine to attach a circular layered cardstock tag to the handle of the reproduction bucket. Tie a bow of brightly colored ribbons around the handle of the matching shovel and this quick and easy dessert is sure to be a hit with kids of all ages!

Bucket-of-Sand Cake

This unique cake is sure to be a hit!

8-inch yellow layer cake, prepared
24-oz. jar applesauce
1 c. vanilla wafers, finely crushed

Cut cake into one-inch cubes. Arrange cubes into a new 8 or 9-cup sand pail lined with plastic wrap, alternating with layers of applesauce. Sprinkle wafer crumbs over top for "sand." Serve with a new sand shovel. Serves 10 to 12.

Beth Kramer
Port Saint Lucie, FL

14

Movie Night Mix

Treat your friends or family to a fun Night at the Movies when you surprise them with bags of Peanut Butter Popcorn. Decorated with advertisements photocopied from vintage magazines, these bags are a snap to make.

Popcorn Bags

Measure the front of your paper bags and size your photocopies to fit; glue the copies to the paper bags. Place the bags of popcorn in the paper bags. Use decorative-edged scissors to cut fold-over toppers from scrapbook paper, staple the toppers over the bags and embellish with scrapbook paper and photocopies of the label, page 46.

Tags

For each tag, photocopy the label and ticket, page 46, onto cardstock and cut out. Center and glue a label to a rectangle of heavy scrapbook paper. Use decorative-edged scissors to trim the short edges of the ticket and tag. Punch a hole in the ticket and tag and tie a length of ribbon through the holes. Add a set of bowls and a much-loved DVD to make a truly memorable gift.

Peanut Butter Popcorn

Quick to make and fast to disappear!

1/2 c. honey
1/2 c. sugar
1/2 t. vanilla extract
1/2 c. creamy peanut butter
2 qts. popped popcorn
mini candy-coated chocolates

Combine honey and sugar over medium heat; bring to a rolling boil. Remove from heat; add vanilla and peanut butter. Drizzle over popped popcorn; toss to mix. Pour onto wax paper and sprinkle with chocolates; cool completely. Place popcorn in plastic zipping bags. Makes about 2 quarts.

Jenny Custis
Lynden, WA

15

Brownie Bites by the Boxful

Everyone loves the chocolatey goodness of fresh-baked brownies! These goodies are even sweeter when presented in cheery containers. Decorate assorted tins and boxes with ribbon, scrapbook paper or cardstock, rickrack, paint or fabric. You can even top your tins with padded lids for a soft and sweet finish.

For a rectangular padded lid, cut a piece of batting the same size as the top of your lid and a piece of fabric 1/2" larger than the batting. Center and layer the batting and fabric on the lid. Working alternately on opposite sides of the rectangle, pull the fabric and glue the raw edges to the sides of the lid. Glue a length of ribbon over the raw edges.

For a round padded lid, cut a circle from cardboard and batting slightly smaller than your lid. Cut a fabric circle 1" larger than the batting and cardboard. Place the fabric circle wrong side up and layer with batting and cardboard. Working alternately on opposite sides of the circle and allowing the fabric to pleat as needed, glue the fabric to the cardboard. Use floss to tightly sew a button to the center of the lid to tuft the padding. Glue the padded circle to the center of the lid.

Accent your containers with vintage buttons and simple monogrammed tags to make these brownie tins the perfect take-home party favor.

From-Scratch Brownies
Just plain delicious!

16-oz. can chocolate syrup
1/2 c. butter
1 c. all-purpose flour
1 c. sugar
4 eggs
non-stick vegetable spray

Mix chocolate syrup, butter, flour and sugar together; add eggs, one at a time, mixing well after each addition. Pour into a greased mini-brownie silicone mold pan containing 24 1 1/2"x1 1/2" molds (or use a 13"x9" baking pan); bake at 350 degrees for 24 to 30 minutes. Makes about 6 dozen mini brownies or 15 to 18 servings in 13"x9" pan.

Jane Davis
Newton, IA

Lemon-Lime Cupcakes

A moist and yummy treat!

18$\frac{1}{4}$-oz. pkg. lemon cake mix
3$\frac{1}{2}$-oz. pkg. instant lemon pudding mix
$\frac{3}{4}$ c. oil
10 oz. lemon lime soda
white decorating icing tinted green, blue
   and yellow and a variety of decorating tips

Mix first 4 ingredients together; fill paper-lined muffin cups $\frac{2}{3}$ full. Bake at 350 degrees for 19 to 23 minutes, or until a toothpick inserted in center comes out clean. Cool and decorate as desired. Refrigerate until ready to serve. Makes 2 dozen.

Mary Thorn
Bloomfield, MO

Celebration Cupcakes

Cupcakes are among the most popular sweet treats, and our Lemon-Lime recipe is sure to become one of your favorites. Decorate each one individually and divide them into just the right number for your gifting needs. Whether given as a single cake on a stand, a foursome in a bakery box or several arranged on a handcrafted tray, these tiny confections say "you're special" to the lucky recipients. Handcrafted tags provide a place to pen a personal note.

Cupcake Stand

This pedestal cupcake stand is really a wooden candleholder, turned upside down and spray painted white. Embellish your cupcake stand with rickrack, velvet ribbon and a Felt Rose then top it with a paper doily. So simple, so sweet!

Cupcake Box

Transform a plain white four-pack bakery box into a cheery gift box. Simply fill the box with cupcakes; then, wrap with a length of wide ribbon, overlapping the ends by 1" at the center back. Glue or tape ends together. Glue a narrow velvet ribbon bow and a Felt Rose to the center front and your sweet treat is ready for giving!

Felt Rose

Use the Rose pattern, page 47, to cut an angled strip of felt. Sew a running stitch along the bottom straight edge of the strip (**Fig. 1**). Beginning with the narrow end and keeping the bottom edge even, pull up the thread to make the felt curl (**Fig. 2**). Adjust the gathers as needed to make a flower shape. Sew through all the layers of the bottom edge several times to hold the flower shape in place; knot and clip the thread ends.

Fig. 1

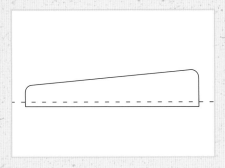

Fig. 2

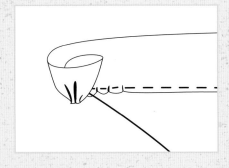

Cupcake Tray & Tag instructions are on page 41.

Chef's Delight

An outdoor chef is sure to be thrilled with this miniature iron skillet filled with our oh-so-easy Onion Butter and an embellished dishtowel.

For the tag, cut a 2½"x4" rectangle from double-sided scrapbook paper. Photocopy the instructions, page 45, onto white cardstock and cut out. Cut a black cardstock rectangle ¼" larger than the instructions. Center, then glue the cardstock rectangle and instructions to the tag. Punch a hole in one corner of the tag and tie it to the skillet handle with jute.

For the towel, cut three lengths of rickrack 1" longer than the width of your towel. Folding the raw ends to the wrong side of the towel, straight stitch the rickrack to the towel. Sew a button to the center of the towel.

  ## Onion Butter
This is so yummy!

¼ c. red onion, grated
¼ c. fresh parsley, minced
¼ c. butter, softened
1 t. Worcestershire sauce
½ t. salt
½ t. pepper
¼ t. dry mustard

Blend all ingredients in a small bowl. Spread over steaks as you remove them from the grill or broiler. Makes about ½ cup.

Jennie Miller
Crystal Beach, FL

Chocolate-Toffee Bites

Crunchy and sweet, they'll never guess the secret ingredient!

saltine crackers
1 c. butter
½ c. sugar
1 c. semi-sweet
   chocolate chips
1 c. chopped walnuts

Line a 15"x10" jelly-roll pan with aluminum foil; cover with a single layer of crackers. Melt butter and sugar in a saucepan; boil for 2 minutes. Pour over crackers; bake at 350 degrees for 10 minutes.

Sprinkle chocolate chips on top; spread when melted. Sprinkle with walnuts and lightly press into chocolate. Refrigerate until cooled.

Break into pieces and store in an airtight container. Makes 25 to 30 servings.

Remona Putman
Rockwood, PA

Perfect Little Bites

Filled with tasty toffee bites, these festive cones bring out the kid in all of us!

Wrap a 10" square of fabric-covered cardstock into a cone shape; glue the edges together. Pink the top edge of the cone and glue rickrack just below the pinked edge. Wrap a pinked 9" paper square into a cone shape and place it in the fabric cone. Fill a cellophane bag with Chocolate-Toffee Bites; tie with ribbons, twill tape and yarn. Add a layered tag embellished with buttons and a pretty lace scrap.

A Clever Notion

Your sewing and crafting friends will be in stitches when you present them with a gift of Almond Button Cookies cleverly packaged in a reproduction vintage button bag.

Matching wrong sides, glue a piece of scrapbook paper and cardstock together; then, cut a 4"x7" backing rectangle. Slip the backing into a 4"x9" clear cellophane treat bag. Fill the bag with Almond Button Cookies. Fold the top of the bag down and staple closed.

Photocopy the Topper, page 43, onto cardstock and cut out. Matching wrong sides and short edges, fold the topper in half and punch a hole where indicated. Write a message on the topper. Slip the topper over the stapled end of the bag and secure with double-stick tape.

Almond Button Cookies
Cute as a button!

½ c. butter, softened
½ c. margarine, softened
½ c. powdered sugar
1 egg
½ t. almond extract
2½ c. all-purpose flour
½ c. almonds, toasted and finely chopped

Blend butter and margarine together in a large bowl. Add powdered sugar, blending until smooth. Add egg and almond extract, mixing well. Stir in flour and almonds.

Roll out dough on a floured surface to ¼-inch thickness and use a 1½-inch diameter cookie cutter to cut out dough. Use a toothpick or small straw to make 2 small holes in center of each cookie. Place on ungreased baking sheets and bake at 350 degrees for 6 to 8 minutes, or until bottoms are lightly browned. Cool on wire racks. Makes about 8 dozen.

Chic Cookie Cans

Do you remember when you were a child how much fun it was to cover a tin can with construction paper to make a pencil holder? Well, these chic cookie cans are simply a grown-up version of that same enjoyable craft! Fill them with Strawberry Delight Cookies to make perfect gifts for your friends!

Measure the circumference of your container and add 1" for overlap. Cut 2 scrapbook paper strips the circumference length which, when added together, equal the total height. Overlapping at center back, glue the strips around the container; embellish with lengths of ribbon and lace. Remove the findings from a piece of vintage jewelry; then, glue it to the center front. Line your container with a linen napkin and fill with cookies.

Tag instructions are on page 41.

Strawberry Delight Cookies

The secret is in the cake mix...it makes these cookies so easy to whip up!

$1/4$ c. butter, softened
8-oz. pkg. cream cheese, softened
1 egg
$1/4$ t. vanilla extract
$18^1/2$-oz. pkg. strawberry cake mix
$3/4$ to 1 c. prepared strawberry frosting

Blend together butter and cream cheese; stir in egg and vanilla. Add dry cake mix one-third at a time, mixing well after each addition. Cover and chill for 30 minutes.

Drop by teaspoonfuls onto ungreased baking sheets. Bake at 375 degrees for 7 to 9 minutes. Microwave frosting for 15 to 30 seconds; drizzle over cooled cookies. Makes 4 dozen.

Moving Day Feast

Mix and match these delicious snack favorites to put together the perfect welcome gift for a new homeowner. Whether you choose to fill a basket or bowl, the Herb Dip, Pita Chips, Herbed Bagel Chips and Seeded Tortilla Crisps are sure to be enjoyed.

Heavenly Herb Dip with Chips

So simple to whip up, and it won't last long.

1 cucumber, peeled and coarsely
    chopped
8 oz. crumbled feta cheese
$\frac{1}{2}$ c. red onion, chopped
1 T. olive oil
$2\frac{1}{2}$ T. lemon juice
3 T. fresh dill, chopped
3 T. fresh mint, chopped

Combine cucumber, cheese and onion in a medium bowl. Sprinkle with oil, lemon juice and herbs; toss to mix. Serve with the following chips and tortilla crisps. Makes 6 servings.

Pita Chips:
3 pita rounds
3 T. olive oil
$\frac{1}{4}$ t. salt
$\frac{1}{4}$ t. pepper

Split pita rounds; cut each round into 8 wedges. Brush oil over both sides of wedges; sprinkle with salt and pepper. Arrange wedges in a single layer on a lightly greased baking sheet. Bake at 375 degrees for 5 minutes on each side, or until crisp. Makes 4 dozen.

Seeded Tortilla Crisps:
$\frac{1}{4}$ c. butter, melted
8 10-inch flour tortillas
$\frac{3}{4}$ c. grated Parmesan cheese
1 egg white, beaten
Seeds: sesame, poppy or
    caraway seed
Seasonings: onion powder,
    cayenne pepper or dried
    cumin to taste
non-stick vegetable spray

Brush butter lightly over one side of each tortilla; sprinkle evenly with cheese and press down lightly. Carefully turn tortillas over. Brush other side with egg white and sprinkle with desired seeds and seasonings. Cut each tortilla into 4 strips with a pastry cutter or knife.

Place strips, cheese-side down, on a baking sheet sprayed with vegetable spray. Bake at 400 degrees, on middle rack of oven, for 8 to 10 minutes, or until crisp and golden. Cool on a wire rack. Makes about $2\frac{1}{2}$ dozen.

Herbed Bagel Chips:
butter-flavored non-stick
    vegetable spray
9 frozen mini bagels, thawed
$1\frac{1}{2}$ t. Italian seasoning
$\frac{1}{4}$ t. onion powder
$\frac{1}{4}$ t. garlic powder
$\frac{1}{8}$ t. cayenne pepper

Spray a baking sheet lightly with vegetable spray; set aside.

Slice each bagel horizontally into 4 slices. Place slices in a single layer on baking sheet and spray lightly with vegetable spray. Combine spices in a jar with a shaker lid; sprinkle over chips. Bake at 375 degrees for 12 minutes or until crisp. Makes 3 dozen.

Welcome Basket, Herb Dip Label, Key Tag, Chip Bags, Welcome Bowl & Bag Toppers instructions begin on page 41.

Flavor-packed Finish

A bright red metal pail makes a colorful container for a hostess gift of Ruby Sauce and a set of crisp white napkins monogrammed with faux redwork. While it might appear that you've spent hours embroidering, the secret is fabric paint applied with a micro tip! A strip of red floral scrapbook paper dresses up the plain white crock of sauce.

Ruby Sauce

Sweet, tart and absolutely the best sauce…you really have to try it on ribs, chicken or pulled pork!

1 c. brown sugar, packed
1 c. sugar
1 c. cider vinegar
1 t. ground ginger
1 t. cinnamon
1 t. allspice
1 t. paprika
½ t. ground cloves
½ t. red pepper flakes
½ t. salt
⅛ t. pepper
2 onions, finely chopped
4 c. rhubarb, finely chopped

Combine all ingredients except onions and rhubarb in a large saucepan over medium heat. Bring to a simmer; stir in onions and rhubarb. Cook for 45 minutes to one hour, or until thickened and rhubarb is tender. Serves 4 to 6.

Jill Valentine
Jackson, TN

Faux Redwork Napkins and Tag

- air-soluble fabric marker
- white fabric napkins
- Plaid® Gallery Glass® Micro Tip Set
- Tulip® fabric paint
- ribbon
- cardstock
- decorative-edged scissors
- scrapbook paper
- craft glue
- 2³⁄₈"x3½" rectangle of self-adhesive felt
- hole punch

Using the fabric marker, trace your desired initial and the flower design, page 44, onto one corner of each napkin. Attach a micro tip to the fabric paint bottle. Following the paint manufacturer's instructions for use, draw over traced lines with short strokes to mimic stitching. Allow paint to dry thoroughly. Tie a ribbon "napkin ring" bow around each napkin.

For the tag, photocopy the label, page 46, onto cardstock and cut out. Use decorative-edged scissors to cut a 3"x4¼" tag from heavy scrapbook paper. Center and glue the label to the felt rectangle; then, adhere the felt rectangle to the tag. Punch a hole in one corner of the tag and tie a ribbon through the hole.

26

RUBY
SAUCE

Try it on ribs, chicken
or pulled pork

Chili Seasoning Mix

You can make several recipes of this mix; it will keep in the freezer.

2 T. chili powder
1 T. dried, minced onion
1 T. dried, minced garlic
2 t. sugar
2 t. ground cumin
2 t. dried parsley
2 t. salt
1 t. red pepper flakes
1 t. dried basil
¹⁄₄ t. pepper

Mix all ingredients together; store in an airtight container. Use 2 tablespoons per pound of ground beef for chili. Makes about ¹⁄₂ cup mix, enough for 2 to 4 batches of chili.

Jill Carr
Carlock, IL

Some Like It Hot

Your family & friends love a good batch of chili so why not share this special blend of spices with a gift of Chili Seasoning Mix? Include a quick, no-sew cook's apron for a truly terrific present.

Seasoning Mix Packet

- Chili Seasoning Mix in a plastic zipping bag
- lunch-size brown paper bag
- double-sided tape
- cardstock
- scrapbook paper
- assorted trims (we used rickrack and ribbon)
- craft glue
- hole punch
- metal charm

Leaving the bottom of the paper bag folded flat toward the back of the bag, use double-sided tape to hold the folded bottom in place. Slip the Seasoning Mix into the paper bag. Fold the top edge over 1$\frac{1}{2}$" toward the front of the bag. Continue folding until the packet measures approximately 5"x5$\frac{1}{2}$". Use double-sided tape to hold the folded top in place.

Photocopy the label, page 46, onto cardstock and cut out. Cut a 4"x5" tag from heavy scrapbook paper. Beginning 1" below one short (top) edge, glue strips of scrapbook paper, ribbon, rickrack and the label to the tag. Center and glue the tag to the front of the packet. Going through all the layers of the bag and tag, punch 2 holes, $\frac{3}{4}$" apart, in the center of the top edge. Working from the back, thread one end of a length of ribbon through each hole. Slip the charm onto the ribbon and tie into a bow at the center front.

Apron

This cheerful red and white apron is oh-sew-easy when you start with an oversized (24"x35") tea towel. Simply fold two corners along one short edge 7" to the wrong side (**Fig. 1**) and secure with fusible web tape. Follow the manufacturer's instructions to attach two $\frac{1}{2}$" diameter grommets where shown in **Fig. 2**. Cut one 78" belt and two 21" neck ties from 1$\frac{1}{4}$" wide twill tape. Insert one raw end of each neck tie through a grommet until there is 2$\frac{1}{2}$" of twill tape showing on the wrong side of the towel; fuse the ends in place. Fold the remaining raw ends of the neck ties and the belt $\frac{1}{4}$" to the wrong side twice and fuse in place. Tie a bow around the folded apron with the belt.

Fig. 1

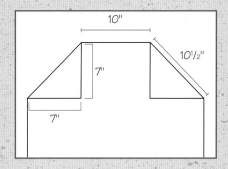

Fig. 2

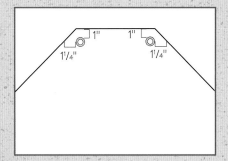

Soup for Everyone

Share some down-home comfort with a gift of Mushroom-Barley Soup, Easy Creamy Potato Soup or Jambalaya Mix. The bags are completely no-sew and the reproduction fabric is reminiscent of the 1930s. Nestle each bag in a large vintage mug for a heart-warming gift.

Mushroom-Barley Soup Mix

You might want to make up several batches... you're sure to get frequent requests!

1/2 c. pearled barley
1/4 c. dried mushroom slices
2 T. dried, minced onion
1/4 c. dried carrot slices
2 T. dried parsley
2 T. dried dill weed
1/2 t. garlic salt
2 bay leaves
2 t. beef bouillon granules

Combine all ingredients in an airtight container; store in a cool, dark place. Give with instructions.

Instructions:

Add mix to one quart boiling water or beef broth; reduce heat and simmer until barley is tender. Remove bay leaves before serving. Makes 4 servings.

Easy Creamy Potato Soup Mix

*Give this mix and you'll
be giving comfort!*

1/4 c. chicken bouillon
　　granules
3 c. instant mashed potato
　　flakes, packed
2 T. dried, minced onion
3 T. dried chives
3/4 t. white pepper
1/4 c. bacon bits
1 T. dried parsley
1 1/2 t. dried dill weed
1/2 t. dried thyme
1 c. powdered milk
1/4 t. paprika

Combine all ingredients;
mix well. Spoon into a plastic
zipping bag. Give with
instructions. Makes about
5 cups mix.

Instructions:

Place 1/2 cup mix into
a soup bowl; add one cup
boiling water. Stir until
smooth and creamy. Garnish
with shredded Cheddar
cheese and bacon bits, if
desired. Makes one serving.

Soup Bags & Instruction Cards
begin on page 42.

Jambalaya Mix

By adding a few ingredients to this dry mix, you will create a hearty meal!

1/2 c. dried sweet pepper flakes
1/4 c. dried, minced onion
1/4 c. dried parsley
1/4 c. beef bouillon granules
3 T. dried minced garlic
1 to 2 T. black pepper
2 T. paprika
1 T. dried oregano leaves
2 t. salt
1 to 2 t. crushed red pepper flakes
1/4 to 1/2 t. cayenne pepper
1/2 t. ground cumin
4 c. white rice, uncooked and divided
4 bay leaves, divided

...smells incredibly good on the stove!

In a medium bowl, combine pepper flakes, onion, parsley, bouillon
granules, garlic, black pepper, paprika, oregano, salt, red pepper
flakes, cayenne and cumin. Place 1 cup rice and 1 bay leaf in each of
4 plastic zipping bags. Divide spice mixture evenly into bags. Seal bags
and give instructions with each gift. Makes about 1 1/2 cups mix.

Instructions:
3 c. water
16 oz. smoked sausage, sliced
14 1/2-oz. can diced tomatoes, undrained
1 bag Jambalaya Mix

In a Dutch oven, bring water, sausage, tomatoes and jambalaya dry
mix to a boil over medium heat, stirring occasionally. Reduce heat to
low. Stirring occasionally, cover and simmer 23 to 28 minutes, or until
most of liquid is absorbed and rice is tender. Remove bay leaf to serve.
Serve warm. Makes 7 cups.

Chill Chaser

No one can resist a mug of steaming hot cocoa on a cold wintry day. For the chocolate lover on your list, pair a jar of great-tasting Back-by -Popular Demand Cocoa Mix with a set of Coasters made from vintage or reproduction fabrics for a chill-chasing treat.

Cocoa Mix Jar, Tag and Bag
- jar of Cocoa Mix
- decorative-edged scissors
- scrapbook paper
- embroidery floss
- buttons
- craft glue
- assorted trims (we used ribbon, twill tape and rickrack)
- hole punch
- 8"x10" brown paper bag with handles
- metal tablespoon with a hole in the handle

For the jar, use decorative-edged scissors to cut a scrapbook paper circle slightly smaller than the top of your jar lid. Use floss to sew a button to the center of the circle. Center and glue the circle to the lid. Glue a length of ribbon around the edge of the lid.

For the tag, cut a 2³/₄"x4¹/₄" and a 2³/₄"x 2" rectangle from heavy scrapbook paper. Use decorative-edged scissors to trim one short (bottom) edge of the larger rectangle; then, glue the smaller rectangle to the top edge. Glue rickrack across the top edge. Punch a hole ¹/₂" below the top edge and tie a length of ribbon through the hole. Use floss to sew a button to the tag. Handwrite the instructions on the tag.

For the bag, glue assorted width strips of scrapbook paper and trims to the front of the bag. Tie twill tape into a bow around the handle. Tie a length of twill tape through the hole in the handle of the measuring spoon. Loop the tag and measuring spoon over the bow.

Coaster instructions are on page 43.

Back-by-Popular-Demand Hot Cocoa Mix

So easy to keep on hand year 'round.

2-lb. pkg. chocolate drink mix
16-oz. jar powdered non-dairy
    creamer
16-oz. pkg. powdered sugar
8-oz. pkg. powdered milk
2 c. mini semi-sweet
    chocolate chips
mini marshmallows

Combine all ingredients except marshmallows; store in an airtight container. Just before giving, place cocoa mix in a jar and add marshmallows on top. Give with instructions. Makes 11 cups mix.

Instructions:

To make a cup of cocoa, stir 3 to 4 tablespoons of mix into 1 cup of boiling water.

Cozy Coffee Break

Visiting a friend for a morning chat will be a real treat when you bring along a gift of Chocolatey Spiced Coffee. An old-fashioned milk bottle and a pretty lidded basket lined with a vintage towel will serve as sweet reminders of those heart-to-heart conversations.

Place a bag of coffee mixture, along with the instructions, in a lunch sack. Trim the sack with a layered cardstock label (photocopy the label on page 46) and some rickrack. Ribbon bows tied through holes punched on the sides keep the sack closed. Layer a ready-made label with cardstock, sign your name and tie to your gift container with ribbon.

Chocolatey Spiced Coffee

This is a dreamy concoction for chocolate and coffee lovers.

Coffee Mixture:
1/2 c. ground coffee
1 1/2 t. cinnamon
1/2 t. nutmeg

Combine all ingredients and place in a resealable plastic zipping bag.

Coffee Flavoring:
1 c. milk
1/2 c. brown sugar, packed
1/3 c. chocolate syrup
1 t. vanilla extract

Combine milk, brown sugar and syrup in a medium saucepan over low heat; cook and stir until sugar dissolves. Stir in vanilla; cool. Pour into a gift container. Keep refrigerated. Give with serving instructions.

Instructions:
Brew coffee mixture with 5 cups of water. Stir brewed coffee and coffee flavoring together. Makes 6 servings.

"Think Green" Food Gift Containers

Coffee Can Treats

An empty coffee can embellished with rolled up tubes made from magazine pages becomes a re-purposed treat can. Line the can with a pretty tea towel and tuck in a cellophane bag of your favorite snack mix for a quick and easy food gift.

If desired, spray paint the inside of your can and allow it to dry.

Cut approximately 75 pages from magazines. Apply a small amount of craft glue along one long end of one page. Beginning with glued end, roll the page around a small dowel or knitting needle making a tube. Glue the opposite end of the page in place and remove the dowel or needle. Repeat to make tubes from the remaining pages.

Measure the height of your can and trim each tube slightly longer than the can height. Hot glue the tubes around the can.

Slip a buckle onto a strip of layered scrapbook paper and glue the strip around the center of the can.

Shoe Box Breakfast Basket

A shoebox becomes a practical basket for a gift of fresh-baked biscuits and a jar of homemade jam. Simply cover the bottom part of a shoebox with wrapping or scrapbook paper and line with a crisp white tea towel. A layered cardstock tag attached with brads is the perfect spot for a handwritten recipe or personal sentiment.

We all want to make our world a cleaner place to live and now you can even go "green" when packaging your food gifts. The eye-catching containers on pages 36-39 are made from everyday household items that might normally be tossed out after their original function is over. The foods items shown are for inspiration only and you are encouraged to use recipes from this book, your favorite family recipes or even purchased food items to fill the containers.

Bottle Cozy

Don't throw away the sweater that kept you warm and cozy for so many years! Recycle it into a snuggly bottle cover! Include a personalized tag and envelope for a one-of-a-kind hostess gift.

Measure the height of your bottle and add 2". Measuring from the finished end of the sleeve, cut a piece of the sleeve the determined measurement. Turn the piece wrong side out. Gather the cut edge and glue or sew to secure; turn right side out. Place the bottle in the sleeve and turn down the cuff. Sew a button to the cuff.

For the tag, cut a 2¹/₄"x4¹/₂" rectangle from heavy scrapbook paper. Punch a hole in the center of one short edge and attach a self-adhesive hole reinforcement. Tie a length of ribbon through the hole. Apply a self-adhesive label to the center of the tag and add a sentiment.

For the envelope, embellish the front of a purchased 2³/₄"x3³/₄" vellum envelope with scrapbook paper, ribbon and a button. Glue a ribbon loop to the back of the envelope. Insert the tag in the envelope and hang over the neck of the bottle.

Treat Bags

If your favorite sweater has a hole or stain that makes it unwearable, give it another function by making Treat Bags from the sleeves. When filled with goodies and tied with a pretty ribbon bow and handcrafted tag, your sweater will continue to bring joy to its lucky new recipient.

For each bag, measure from the finished end of one sleeve and cut a piece 11" long. Turn the piece wrong side out. Sew the raw edges together; turn right side out. Place a cellophane bag filled with goodies in the treat bag and tie closed with a length of ribbon. Fold the cuff down.

For each tag, glue scrapbook paper, ribbon and a button onto a purchased 2¹/₄"x3³/₄" hang tag. Glue a piece of pre-punched scrapbook paper to a purchased 1¹/₄"x1³/₄" mini hang tag. Handwrite a special message on the small tag. Layer, then insert a length of ribbon through the holes in both tags and tie to the ribbon on the bag.

Fun Party Pops
(also shown on page 6)

Slip each Chocolatey Rice Pop into a clear cellophane treat bag and close with a twist tie. Tie one pop on each paddle with a ribbon bow. Wrap the elastic string around the paddle and pop; then, tuck the ball under the string at the center front.

Break Bread Together
(also shown on page 7)
Dipping Sauce Jar

Use decorative-edged scissors to cut a 2¼"x2¼" square of scrapbook paper. Photocopy the label, page 45, onto cardstock and cut out. Insert the label into the metal-rimmed tag; then, attach the tag to the square of scrapbook paper using the brads. Glue the label on the jar. Tie a length of ribbon around the jar lid. "Sew" a

length of narrow ribbon through the buttonholes; then, glue the button over the knot.
Tag

Cut a 2½"x4½" rectangle from cardstock and scrapbook paper. Glue the scrapbook paper and cardstock rectangles together. Use decorative-edged scissors to trim one end of the tag and punch a hole in the opposite end. On the trimmed end, glue lengths of ribbon, rickrack and lace edging to the tag. Write a message on the hang tag; then, tie the tag and hang tag together with ribbon and twill tape.

A Sweet Surprise
(also shown on page 9)
Salsa Jar

For the jar topper, cut one circle from cardboard (slightly smaller than your jar lid) and another from batting. Cut a circle from cardstock ½" smaller than the cardboard circle. Cut a circle from embroidered linen 1" larger than the cardboard circle. Place the fabric circle wrong side up and layer batting and cardboard on top. Working alternately on opposite sides of the circle and allowing the fabric to pleat as needed, glue the fabric to the cardboard. Glue the cardstock circle over the raw edges

of the fabric. Glue the topper to the jar lid.

Photocopy the Apple-Berry Salsa label, page 45, onto cardstock and cut out. Using decorative-edged scissors, cut a cardstock rectangle 2¾"x1¾". Layer and glue the label and cardstock rectangle together. Glue the layered rectangles to the scrapbook paper jar label. Punch a hole in each short end of the jar label; apply self-adhesive hole reinforcements. Tie the label to the jar using a length of ribbon threaded through the holes. Glue a length of ribbon around the neck of the jar.

A Peach of a Gift
(also shown on page 12)
Tag

Cut a rectangle the same size as your tag from an embroidered section of a napkin. Glue the rectangle to the tag. Photocopy the label, page 45, onto cardstock and cut out. Using decorative-edged scissors, cut a rectangle from scrapbook paper ½" larger than the label. Layer and glue the label and rectangle to the tag. Embellish the tag with ribbon and buttons.

Celebration Cupcakes

(also shown on page 18)

Cupcake Tray

- Lemon-Lime Cupcakes
- white spray paint
- picture frame
- cardboard cut to fit in your frame
- scrapbook paper
- craft glue
- 2-part epoxy
- 2 drawer handles
- assorted ribbon

Remove the glass and backing from the frame. Spray paint the frame and cardboard. Glue scrapbook paper to one side of the cardboard. Insert the glass, cardboard and backing into the frame. Center and use epoxy to glue one handle to each end of the frame. Tie a bow on one handle and arrange the cupcakes on the tray for a gift of sweet indulgence.

Tags

For the rectangular tag (shown with the cupcake stand), cut a rectangle from scrapbook paper. Glue a purchased decorative-edged tag to the rectangle. Embellish a small hang tag with ribbon, rickrack and a button; then, clip it to the rectangle with a mini clothespin.

For the round tag (shown with the cupcake box), use decorative-edged scissors to cut a circle from scrapbook paper; punch a hole close to the edge. Use ribbon to tie a purchased decorative-edged tag to the circle and clip on a mini clothespin.

For the large hang tag (shown with the cupcake tray), start with a purchased 2½"x4" hang tag. Glue strips of scrapbook paper, ribbon, rickrack, cotton lace and a button to the tag.

Add hand-written sentiments to complete your Tags.

Chic Cookie Cans

(also shown on page 23)

Tags

For the "Mary" tag, glue strips of ribbon, scrapbook paper, lace and beaded trim across the bottom edge of a purchased hang tag. Use the small hang tag pattern, page 46, to cut a small tag from heavy scrapbook paper; then, use decorative-edged scissors to trim the bottom edge. Punch a hole in the center of the top; then, write your message on the tag. Tie the two tags together with lengths of narrow ribbon.

For the "envelope" tag, glue strips of ribbon, scrapbook paper and lace across the front of a purchased 2¾"x3¾" mini envelope. Cut a 2¼"x2¾" rectangle from cardstock and embellish one short end with a circular sticker. Punch a hole though the center of the sticker and tie a ribbon through the hole. Write a sentiment on the tag and slip the tag in the envelope.

Moving Day Feast

(also shown on page 24)

Welcome Basket

A wire basket lined with crisp linen tea towels holds a vintage jar filled with Herb Dip and bags of Pita and Herbed Bagel Chips. The handcrafted Key Tag provides a place for a special message.

- jar of Herb Dip
- cellophane bags of Pita and Herbed Bagel Chips
- craft glue
- scrapbook paper
- decorative-edged scissors
- cardstock
- 1½" diameter metal-rimmed circle tags

Instructions continued on page 42.

- assorted trims (we used ribbon, twill tape, rickrack and string)
- hole punch
- metal grommet with a $\frac{1}{2}$" diameter opening
- $\frac{7}{8}$" diameter button
- $2\frac{1}{2}$"x4" hang tag
- vintage house key
- brown paper bags
- wire basket
- linen tea towels

Herb Dip Label

Match wrong sides and glue two 2"x2" pieces of scrapbook paper together. Trim two sides with decorative-edged scissors. Photocopy the label, page 45, onto cardstock; cut out and glue to the center of a metal-rimmed tag. Tie twill tape around the jar and attach the layered and punched tag to the ribbon with string.

Key Tag

Cut a 3"x7" tag from cardstock. Cover the tag with assorted scraps of scrapbook paper and ribbon trims. Attach a grommet to one end of the tag. Layer, then glue the button and metal-rimmed tag to the opposite end. Tie assorted ribbons, twill tape and rickrack through the grommet.

Photocopy the label, page 45, onto cardstock and cut out using decorative-edged scissors. Cut a $2\frac{1}{4}$" diameter circle from cardstock. Layer, then glue the circles to the hang tag. Use ribbon to tie the key onto the hang tag; then, loop the ribbon over the tag.

Chip Bags

Glue twill tape, rickrack and strips of scrapbook paper to the front of the brown bags; trim the top edge with decorative-edged scissors. Tie a ribbon around the top of each cellophane chip bag. Photocopy the labels, page 45; cut out and glue to the center of the metal-rimmed tags. Use narrow ribbon to tie the tags to the cellophane bags and place inside the decorated bags.

Welcome Bowl

Once a part of a set of four, this orphaned mixing bowl takes on a new role when it becomes a serving bowl for a housewarming gift of chips, crisps and assorted beverages.

- Herbed Bagel Chips and Seeded Tortilla Crisps in cellophane bags
- vintage mixing bowl
- $5\frac{1}{4}$"x$8\frac{1}{2}$" brown paper bags
- stapler
- craft glue
- scrapbook paper
- decorative-edged scissors
- cardstock
- assorted trims (we used ribbon, twill tape and rickrack)
- buttons
- embroidery floss
- miniature clothespins

Bag Toppers

Place chips in brown paper bags and staple to close. Cut two 6"x$6\frac{1}{2}$" rectangles from scrapbook paper. Glue ribbon, rickrack and strips cut from scrapbook paper across one short end of each rectangle; then, trim ends using decorative-edged scissors. Match short ends and fold toppers in half.

For the tags, photocopy the labels, page 45, onto cardstock and cut out. Embellish the tags with ribbons and buttons. Use floss to sew each button and tag to a length of twill tape. Place a topper and tag over the stapled edge of each bag and secure with a miniature clothespin.

Soup for Everyone
(also shown on page 30)

Soup Bags & Instruction Cards
- Mushroom-Barley Soup, Easy Creamy Potato Soup or Jambalaya Mix in a plastic zipping bag
- one 7"x21" rectangle of fabric for each bag
- stapler
- twill tape
- buttons
- craft glue
- cardstock

Instructions continued on page 43.

For each bag, match wrong sides and short edges to fold the fabric rectangle in half. Spacing staples about ¹/₂" apart, staple along each long edge of the rectangle. Turn right side out and insert a bag of soup mix. Tie twill tape into a bow around the bag and glue a button over the knot.

For each instruction card, photocopy the instructions, page 47, onto white cardstock and cut out. Cut a 5¹/₄"x3¹/₄" rectangle from brightly colored cardstock. Center and glue the instructions to the cardstock rectangle.

For each coaster, place one fabric square wrong side up; then, center and layer one batting and one cardboard square on top. Working alternately on opposite sides of the square, glue the raw edges of the fabric to the

cardboard. Use floss to sew a button to the center of the square. Use decorative-edged scissors to cut four 4¹/₂"x4¹/₂" squares from felt. Center and glue one fabric square on each felt square.

A Clever Notion
(page 22)

Chill Chaser
(also shown on page 32)
Coasters
Supplies and instructions are for four coasters
• four 4¹/₂"x4¹/₂" squares of fabric
• four 3³/₄"x3³/₄" squares of batting
• four 3³/₄"x3³/₄" squares of heavy cardboard
• craft glue
• embroidery floss
• 4 buttons
• decorative-edged scissors
• 9"x9" square of felt

The FASHION

A Sweet Surprise
(page 9)

apple-berry salsa

A Sweet Surprise
(page 9)

cinnamon
chips
for
dipping

Moving Day Feast
(page 24)

pita
chips

bagel
chips

herb
dip

Moving Day Feast
(page 24)

Welcome
Home

**Break Bread
Together**
(page 7)

Dipping
Sauce

A Peach of a Gift
(page 12)

Spiced
Peaches

Moving Day Feast
(page 24)

herbed
bagel
chips

Moving Day Feast
(page 24)

seeded
tortilla
crisps

Chef's Delight
(page 20)

Onion Butter

Spread over steaks as you remove
them from the grill or broiler.

Movie Night Mix
(page 14)

Peanut Butter Popcorn

Movie Night Mix
(page 14)

Welcome to:

Sunday
Night
at the
Movies

Movie Night Mix
(page 14)

Chic Cookie Cans
(page 23)

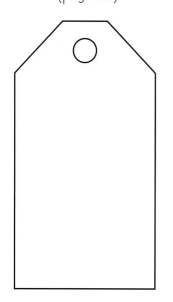

Cozy Coffee Break
(page 34)

COFFEE

Flavor-packed Finish
(page 27)

RUBY
SAUCE

Try it on ribs, chicken
or pulled pork

Some Like It Hot
(page 28)

Chili Seasoning Mix
Add 2 T. to one pound of ground beef

rose pattern

Easy Creamy Potato Soup Mix

Instructions:

Place ¹/₂ cup mix into a soup bowl; add one cup boiling water. Stir until smooth and creamy. Garnish with shredded Cheddar cheese and bacon bits, if desired. Makes one serving.

Mushroom-Barley Soup Mix

Instructions:

Add mix to one quart boiling water or beef broth; reduce heat and simmer until barley is tender. Remove bay leaves before serving. Makes 4 servings.

Jambalaya Mix

Instructions:
3 c. water
16 oz. smoked sausage, sliced
14¹/₂-oz. can diced tomatoes, undrained
1 bag Jambalaya Mix

In a Dutch oven, bring water, sausage, tomatoes and jambalaya dry mix to a boil over medium heat, stirring occasionally. Reduce heat to low. Stirring occasionally, cover and simmer 23 to 28 minutes, or until most of liquid is absorbed and rice is tender. Remove bay leaf to serve. Serve warm. Makes 7 cups.

Credits

Production Team:
Instructional Writer - Jean Lewis
Technical Editor - Laura Siar Bertram
Editorial Writers - Jean Lewis and Susan McManus Johnson
Senior Graphic Artist - Lora Puls
Graphic Artist - Angela Ormsby Stark
Production Artists - Dayle Carozza, Dana Vaughn
and Janie Marie Wright
Photo Stylist -Christy Myers
Photographer - Mark Mathews
Special Projects Designer - Patti Uhiren
Foods Editor - Jane Kenner Prather
Contributing Test Kitchen Staff - Rose Glass Klein
and Celia Berry Martin

We have made every effort to ensure that these recipes and instructions are accurate and complete. We cannot, however, be responsible for human error, typographical mistakes, or variations in individual work.